Science and Spirituality

Copyright 2016 John A. Ryan

All rights reserved. No part of this publication may be reproduced, stored in a retrieval system, or transmitted in any from or by any means, electronic, mechanical, photocopying, recording or otherwise without prior permission from the publishers.

Published by
Mzuni Press
P/Bag 201 Luwinga
Mzuzu 2

ISBN 978-99960-27-01-7
Mzuni Texts no. 1

The Mzuni Press is represented outside Africa by:
African Books Collective Oxford (order@africanbookscollective.com)

www.mzunipress.luviri.net
www.africanbookscollective.com

Science and Spirituality

John A. Ryan

Mzuni Texts no.1

Mzuni Press

Mzuzu

2016

Table of Contents

Introduction	4
Chapter 1: Science vs Religion	5
The Clash of Science and Religion	5
The Logic behind the Clash	6
Chapter 2: Science	8
The Building Blocks of All Matter	8
Scientific Method	9
Objectivity in Science	9
The Benefits Science Brought	10
The Misery that Science Brought	11
Chapter 3: Spirituality, Religion and Theology	13
Recent Developments in Theology	15
Chapter 4: What is Quantum?	18
Our Limited Vision	18
Three Levels of World	19
The Quantum World	19
Chapter 5: Mathematics and the Quantum	21
Some Thoughts on Mathematics	21
The Mathematics Used in Describing the Quantum World	22
The Fuzziness of the Quantum World	24

Chapter 6: Science and Quantum 26
- Wave or Particle 26
- A Bundle of Energy in Relationship 26
- Einstein's Theory of Relativity 27
- Einstein and Mathematics 27
- The Mystics Always Had a Glimpse of these Realities 28

Chapter 7: Experiments in Science 29
- The Double Slit Experiment 29
- The Entanglement Experiment 29
- No Such Thing as a Neutral Observer 30
- Quantum Computers 31
- The Potential of Quantum Computers 32
- Post Quantum Cryptography Research
  at Mzuzu University 32

Chapter 8: Implications of the New Science 33
- The Relatedness of Everything 33
- A Participatory World 33
- Environmental Issues 34
- The GAIA Hypothesis 34
- A New Mindset 34
- New Revelation 35
- Redemption of All of Creation 36

Chapter 9: Our Response. 38
- Celebrate through Rhythm and Dance 38
- Mathematics Having the Final Word 38

Introduction

I feel excited. As a priest in the Catholic Church, I have had a wonderful opportunity of promoting the Spiritual in our lives for over 30 years now. As a person who enjoys Mathematics I have had the joy of passing on this passion to others. Sometimes people ask me 'how did you as a Missionary Priest get so heavily involved in promoting Mathematics?' I answer something like 'The Mission to spread the Kingdom of God and the Mission of passing on a passion for Mathematics is the same for me'. I emphasise **for me**. For others it could be hospital work, for yet others it could be building churches, etc etc. God has deposited a variety of gifts in his people and he expects each to use their gifts for the building up of His Kingdom.

The beauty and elegance found in Mathematics has always pointed me to the Divine and, in my own mind, I never saw any division. However, it was not always easy to communicate this 'oneness' to others. Now, for the first time, with the elegant mathematics involved in the Quantum World, it is becoming easier to communicate some of the riches and wonderment exposed to one who pursues Mathematics. In the same process, the apparent divide which has existed between Science and Religion is being obliterated. The exciting element is that, it is possible to communicate a lot of this in non technical terms and so make it accessible to the non mathematician and to a far wider audience. I do hope that the reader will be enriched by the following pages.

Chapter 1: Science versus Religion

1. The Clash of Science and Religion

The Institute of Electrical and Electronic Engineers[1] (IEEE) is one of the largest and most respected professional bodies in the scientific world and Spectrum Radio[2] is its official on line radio station. On Spectrum Radio, in April 2009, Steven Cherry interviewed Robert Park who is Professor of Physics at the University of Maryland in the USA about his views on Science and Belief in God. In the interview Park says

> What troubles me the most is the fact that some scientists are believers. I find that very hard to understand. That you can be a scientist and compartmentalize your beliefs so thoroughly—on the one side you use one set of rules to draw conclusions and then on the other side you use an entirely different set of rules, a contradictory set of rules, to draw other conclusions.

Robert Park is a product of the education system during the latter half of the twentieth century where Science and Religion misunderstood each other. Science and Religion seemed to be disciplines belonging to different worlds. Many people, like Robert Park, felt that they were irreconcilable. In this paper we show how Science and Religion are now coming to the same conclusions using different paths.

---

[1] http://www.ieee.org/
[2] http://spectrum.ieee.org/

2. The Logic behind the Clash

It is clear that Robert Park expects everything to follow the same set of rules, the same set of logical argument and the same route as mapped out by the physical laws of science, by the Law of Gravity, by Newton's Laws of Motion, by Boyle's Law for Gases etc. One set of rules applies to all of reality. One set of rules explains all of reality. One set of rules directs all of reality. One set of rules fits all.

The set of rules that Robert Park is talking about originates from the systematic deductive logic as first developed by Aristotle who was born in 384 BC and died in 322 BC.[3] Aristotle believed that logic is the basis of all Science and he was the first to propose that each branch of Science should begin with its own set of axioms, an accepted set of principles from which everything else is deduced. Aristotle himself did not use the term 'logic' but talked about 'analytics' and developed the famous ' Prior Analytics' which consists of two premises and a conclusion as in the following example, which was given by Aristotle himself:

- Every Greek is a person
- Every person is mortal
  Therefore every Greek is mortal.[4]

This systematic deductive logic became supreme in all of scientific thought, scientific investigation and scientific development. Science here is used in its widest sense, including disciplines like Sociology and Philosophy. Aristotle also saw logic as uniting all of knowledge and saw mathematics, philosophy and physics as

---

[3] http://www.bookrags.com/biography/aristotle/
[4] http://ebooks.adelaide.edu.au/a/aristotle/a8pra/

different faces of one reality. Aristotle did not separate different scientific disciplines into different boxes but realised that all areas of life were connected and interconnected. Plato's Academy,[5] which Aristotle helped to develop, was not only devoted to mathematics and science but also philosophy, religion and politics, as all were seen as related. However, it is in more recent times that knowledge was boxed and parcelled in separate compartments and as Science tried to specialize more and more, this compartmentalising reached extremes.

On the other hand Robert Park sees 'Belief in God' as belief on the basis of submission to a higher authority with no reference to logical argument or rational discourse. For him such a 'Belief' is 'ill-informed'. An entirely 'different set of rules' is applied in its justification. The fact that such a 'Belief in God' cannot be 'objectively proven beyond doubt' using systematic deductive logic is a problem for him. The 'Belief in God' does not stand up to the scrutiny of scientific investigation which follows one set of rules which include the laws of deductive logic, Newton's Laws of Motion, Boyle's Law for Gases etc. For Robert Park everything has to follow this one set of rules.

We are merely taking Robert Park as an example of the all too common position taken by many in the academic world during the latter part of the last century when 'Belief in God' was often seen as incompatible with scientific experiment and scientific rigour.[6] But this need not be the case.

---

[5] http://en.wikipedia.org/wiki/Platonic_Academy
[6] John Polkinghorne, *Quantum Physics and Theology*, Yale University Press, 2007.

Chapter 2: Science

1. The Building Blocks of All Matter

The process of compartmentalisation of knowledge was given great impetus by another concept which crept into scientific thought and research, namely the idea of breaking down a thing into its constituent parts and seeing an entity as merely the sum of its parts. Full knowledge of a thing could be gained by breaking it down into simpler parts, knowing the makeup of the simpler parts and then putting the parts together to make the whole. This model works well for a machine or a computer. Computer repair, in fact, is merely about identifying one of the six or seven parts of a computer which is not functioning properly and then replacing that part. The model works well for a bicycle. Again, identify the part giving problems, replace it and the bicycle is ready again for cycling. It is this very model which motivated scientists to search for the basic building blocks of all matter. Perhaps this idea came originally from Plato who believed everything was made from four elements, namely earth, fire, air and water.[7] They were referred to as the 'Platonic solids'. By the beginning of the twentieth century, this list was replaced by another list of 103 elements which were considered indivisible and all matter was constituted from these 103 elements.[8] Again, the idea was that full understanding of matter could be gained by breaking it down into its constituent parts. Emphasis is placed on full knowledge of the individual parts. Then simply adding up or putting together the well known and well researched individual parts gives rise to full knowledge of matter in its different forms. Therefore much effort

---

[7] http://en.wikipedia.org/wiki/Platonic_solids
[8] http://www.periodic-table.com/

is placed on isolating the individual parts and attaining 'full knowledge' about them and of them.

2. Scientific Method

This 'isolating individual parts' or 'extracting specific situations' has been the approach of Science in all its forms up to the present day. First one isolates a situation, puts restrictions and clearly defined limits on it and then analyses it in minute detail and in depth. This method has been applied not only in the empirical sciences but also in the social sciences, in philosophy, in theology and in all of life situations. It is an effort to simplify life situations and bring them to manageable portions which can then be analysed and controlled. It is an effort to be in charge of life situations, to be able to manipulate and dominate the processes of life. This was epitomised by the French mathematician, Pierre Laplace, in the 19th century when he said:

> An intelligence knowing all forces acting in nature as well as knowing the positions of all things—to it nothing would be uncertain, both future and past would be present before its eyes. [9]

In the last couple of centuries this linear logic and this scientific method of breaking things down into smaller and simpler parts was seen as the tool not only for understanding all of reality but for fixing all problems and for making progress in all of life situations.

3. Objectivity in Science

Objective truth has become the bedrock of all progress where having isolated a situation, definite 'objective' conclusions are

---

[9] Quoted in *Superforce* by Paul Davies, London Unwin Books, 1984

derived and these 'objective' conclusions are given a prominence and a permanency associated with the word 'objective'. Intuition and imagination have no role to play in serious science or in serious research. Everything has to be 'objective' and 'proven beyond doubt' in order to gain the respect of the scientific community. Everything has to follow the linear logic of Aristotle and fit in with the Law of Gravity or Newton's Laws of Motion or Boyle's Law etc. Rational is the word which must apply to all scientific investigation if it is to be credible or accepted by the scientific community or if it is to be accepted as 'objective'.

4. The Benefits Science Brought

There is no doubt that such 'objective' science has brought benefits to humankind on planet Earth. Especially in Western Europe and in the United States of America as well as in other 'developed' countries, the drudgery has been taken out of the daily struggle to feed, clothe and house oneself with the result of much longer life spans for many. Mechanisation in farming has increased food production several times over. Motor cars and airplanes, roads and airports have made travel easy and comfortable. The advances in telecommunications in recent years have allowed us to be in constant contact with one another despite being physically separated by big distances. Television, radio and iPods are opening up many opportunities and possibilities for humans. The list goes on and on. We could easily fill pages describing the benefits brought to human kind by Science. Notice I say 'benefits to **human kind'**, I am not claiming any benefits for animals or for the flowers, for the forests, for the rivers, for the wetlands, for the seas, for the fish, for the birds, for the air etc.

5. The Misery that Science Brought

But Science has also brought misery and destruction to some of humankind. The thirst to dominate and control, as inspired by Science, has given way to much war and strife. The proliferation of arms in the world, especially in the less developed countries, is giving rise to a lot of crime and insecurity. Weapons of mass destruction have not only decimated large populations with continuing cancerous and deadly infections for present and future generations but are also a constant threat to our survival on planet Earth. Drugs, modern technology and greed have brought great sophistication into crime throughout the developed world posing great challenges to policing and law enforcing agents. Children can no longer roam freely in playful abandonment but have to be constantly supervised by known and trusted adults. Population explosion is also posing huge challenges. At the present rate of population growth, a billion people are being added to planet Earth every 30 years. For the first time ever, the continent of Africa is now supporting one billion people. This together with climate change, deforestation, depletion of soils, droughts, use of chemicals, etc is perpetuating and propagating further poverty and misery in many people's lives. The exploitation of women, human trafficking and prostitution are increasing at alarming rates everywhere throughout the world through the various means of modern technology. Young minds are being poisoned with pornography both in print and electronic forms. The air, the rivers, the seas, the mountains, the plains, the lakes, the wetlands, the bogs, etc are being polluted with toxic chemicals due to modern methods of farming and mass industrial means of production. The list goes on and on.

It is the same mechanistic model of Science and the same Aristotelian logic which is allowing the rich to become richer at the expense of the poor. The economic gap between those who are accumulating vast material resources for themselves and those who live on the edge in isolated areas of the world is widening. Those who are doing the accumulating for themselves are changing the climate in isolated areas resulting (for example in some cases) in drought where essential crops fail, giving rise to poverty, sicknesses, starvation and death. And then when the international aid agencies come in with emergency help, which is not only necessary but essential, the spirit of self reliance is destroyed and replaced by a dependency syndrome further perpetuating the economic inequity. Those who leave the isolation of rural areas and congregate in urban ghettos, suffer not only from economic inequities but also from social inequities. The scale and experience of inequity is exacerbated giving rise to even more social problems. The list goes on and on.

Chapter 3: Spirituality, Religion and Theology

1. Spirituality, Religion and Theology

Let us begin this chapter by exploring what we mean by the three terms (a) Spirituality, (b) Religion and (c) Theology.

    a. Spirituality is the quest for meaning in life. It is inherent in the human condition. It asks the major life questions like: Where did we come from? Where are we going? What is the meaning of life? What am I here for? Humans have grappled with these questions from the beginning of human history, nearly 100,000 years ago. When our ancient ancestors offered sacrifices to the gods in the mountains or in the forests they were taking part in this quest for meaning in life. We are still grappling with these questions today. The search takes many and varied forms. Many search within the established religions and churches. Others search outside these structures. When people climb Kaning'ina mountain to pray all night they are partaking in this very search. When people gather together to sing, dance and speak in tongues they are also partaking in this search. Some would say the indulging in drugs, sex and alcohol is a misguided effort in this search, an effort which of course only leads to destruction and emptyness. Spirituality is as varied as there are people and as old as humanity itself.

b. Religion, on the other hand, is a recent visitor to our planet. All the major religions have their origins within the last 5,000 years. Different religions may have very different origins but, in general, Religion does organise, direct and shape Spirituality, it gives it a context within which to express it, to celebrate it and explore it further. Some have observed that the major religions came within the period of the agricultural revolution (the last 10,000 years) when planet earth was divided up and further divided and subdivided into different countries, regions, districts, estates, farms etc and when boundaries and borders were constructed and peoples claimed ownership and sovereignty over parcels of land and water. The advent of religions came within the era of this parcelling and subdividing and ordering of property and agriculture and livlihoods. O'Murchu poses the question: "Was Religion also an effort to organise and even control spirituality?"[10]

c. The word 'Theology' comes from the two Latin words 'Theos' meaning God and 'Logos' meaning word. In Christian circles, at least up to 1200 AD, theology was mainly about interpreting the Bible and in particular the four Gospels of the New Testament within the tradition of the Christian Church founded by Jesus. Theology was seen as bringing out the deeper meaning of these books and

---

[10] Diarmud O'Murchu, *Quantum Theology*, Crossroad Publishing, New York, 2004, Chapter 2.

their practical implications for daily life of the Christian faithful. Around the thirteenth century Thomas Acquinas broadened this understanding of Theology saying Theology was 'Faith Seeking Understanding'. Then, after the Reformation period and the establishment of the Protestant Churches, the Protestant Churches continued an allegiance to the Bible as the supreme authority while the Catholic Church developed a sacramental and canonical approach. Theology then was developed as particular traditions within particular churches giving rise to different theologies.

2. Recent Developments in Theology[11]

In more recent times the focus of Theology was further broadened with the recovery of the real meaning of the term 'Word' as translated from the Hebrew 'Dabhar'; Dabhar meaning that Divine Creative Energy which was there from the beginning. In the beginning of John's Gospel we read "In the beginning was the Word and the Word was with God and the Word was God." The 'Word' here has a very rich meaning — that Divine Creative Intelligence, Creative Wisdom, Creative Energy, which was there in the beginning, there throughout all of the billions of years of history of the universe, continually creating, continually shaping, continually transforming and still there now continuing to create, shape and transform everything. St Paul says "All of creation is groaning in one great act of giving birth."[12] The churches continually talk about 'saving and renewing' bringing about a 'new

---

[11] Diarmud O'Murchu, *Quantum Theology*, Crossroad Publishing, New York, 2004, Chapter 2.
[12] Romans 8:22

heaven and a new earth'. So Theology now is seen as exploring that Divine Dabhar which continues to create, to sustain and to transform. Theology is no longer the preserve of any one church or one tradition but now even explores ways and means of bringing all these diverse traditions closer together, recognizing that no one tradition contains all the wisdom but that the fuller picture is found in the diversity of all traditions. So in recent times different strains of Theology have emerged. Among the different strains are:

   a. Liberation Theology: A Christian Theology more about liberation in this world than salvation in a life to come. It is very pragmatic, it considers the system and the structural oppression and it seeks political change and changes in the structure. It is not a top down approach but begins with human beings in their daily life struggle.
   b. Feminist Theology: It is not just about ordination of women but treats far more fundamental questions and challenges patriarchy and sexism. It seeks to overcome the traditional dualism of emotions vs intellect, heart vs head, irrational vs rational. The emphasis is on being holistic, inclusive and in harmony.
   c. Creation Theology: Traditionally theology considered the world to be a transitory place, not worthy of deep trust and love. The world was identified with planet Earth. The 'End of the World' loomed large in traditional theology. Now we are far more knowledgable about the origins of not only planet Earth but of the whole universe, we are invited to confront our

anthropocentrism (seeing things only from the human point of view), we realize that we share this world and this universe with many other creatures, we are invited to examine our 'world denouncing spirituality', to reverse our 'masculine tendencies to dominate', to halt the 'manipulation and the exploitation of creation' for human benefit. We are invited to see the bigger picture, our place in that bigger picture and thus bow down in respect and homage before it all.

d. Inter-Church Theology: Inter-Church Theology is raising many intruiging questions. All religions are attempts to interpret and contextualize God's revelation to Humanity. The possibility that religions belong to the Age of Patriarchy and to the Age of the Agricultural Revolution (8,000 BC -2,000 AD) and may have diminished importance as we move into a new evolutionary epoc may need to be examined further in the light of the present decline of religious practice in many parts of the 'developed' world. In the past Religion was the main way in which people explored and articulated their spiritual desires while today people are doing it in other ways.

Chapter 4: What is Quantum?

1. Our Limited Vision

We live in a world which we experience with our five senses of hearing, seeing, smelling, tasting and touching. We are limited by these five senses. A fish that lives its whole life in water has no idea and no picture of what the lake looks like from the mountains. The fish probably cannot even imagine what is not water. The fact that it lives all its life in water limits its understanding to 'water things' and it has no idea of what is 'outside water'. We humans are no different. We literally find it difficult to see 'beyond our noses'. We are limited because we can only 'see' with our ears, eyes, nose, tongue (to taste) and hand (to touch). We cannot see that space and time are just different sides of one thing and maybe not even different sides but as Einstein said just 'one continuum'—the space time continuum, something which is far bigger than what we can imagine, something which envelops us and envelops our whole world. And since we live all our lives 'in the water' we are unable to see the mountains and unable to see the lake from the mountains. We are unable to see and experience the space time continuum.

Nor can we see or feel or smell or taste or touch the smallest pieces of matter which make up our bodies and make up the world we live in. We only experience the 'middle world', the world which consists of:

- things which are far bigger than atoms and electrons (those things which we can experience, can see, can touch, can smell, can taste, can hear) and

- things which are far smaller than the larger realities like the space time continuum.

2. Three Levels of World

We have then three realities or three levels of world:

1. The Microscopic World made up of quarks, electrons, atoms etc. The Microscopic World is real but not immediately accessible to our senses.
2. The Middle World made up of things which we can experience and where we exist. The Middle World is available to our senses.
3. The Macro World which envelops us. The Macro World is real but not immediately accessible to our senses.

3. The Quantum World

Quantum is about the Microscopic World. Quantum Physics explores the realities of the microscopic world. Quantum Mechanics tries to manipulate the microscopic world. Quantum Mathematics describes the microscopic world. Quantum Theology explores the spiritual implications of the new knowledge of the microscopic world. Entering into the microscopic world is entering a world unknown to us, a world which (despite the fact that it provides the building blocks of all of reality as we know it) does not obey the laws of the middle world. It is a world which baffles us. It is a world which does not follow 'our logic'. It is a world of mystery. It is a world of fascination. It is beyond our understanding, beyond our dreams and beyond our imaginings. Niels Bohr, who won the Nobel Prize for Physics in 1922, said "He who is not shocked by the Quantum World does not understand it."[13] We are only beginning to realise how mysterious it all is. Yet entering into the microscopic world gives us a better understanding of the middle world. It in fact changes our 'world view'.

---

[13] http://nobelprize.org/nobel_prizes/physics/laureates/1922/bohr-bio.html

Chapter 5: Mathematics and the Quantum

1. Some Thoughts on Mathematics

Some confuse mathematics with numbers. Numbers are used in many disciplines, e.g. accountancy, engineering, history, geography, and mathematics is just another discipline where numbers are sometimes used. Numeracy would be a better word to describe one's familiarity with numbers, one's ability to manipulate numbers or one's ability to crunch numbers. Mathematics, on the other hand, is about structures, describing structure, analysing structure and appreciating structure. Mathematics is sometimes perceived to be abstract as many of its concepts cannot be directly seen. However, what is making Mathematics so intriguing now is the fact that some of the abstract structures which have been developed over the years (developed as abstract structures for their own beauty and elegance) are now those very structures which describe the Quantum World. Abstract Mathematics is now the only tool available to explore, describe and manipulate the Quantum World, a real world. The question may be asked 'Is it proper to continue to call this mathematics abstract'? However, let us not get bogged down in semantics. It is worth pointing out that this mathematics, which is so accurate in describing the Quantum World, was initially perused for its own intrinsic beauty and elegance. Paul Dirac, who at the age of 31 years won the 1933 Nobel Prize in Physics, once wrote "It is more important to have beauty in one's equations than for the equations to fit experiment".[14] Beauty and elegance have always been considered as a yardstick for the correctness of mathematics.

---

[14] http://en.wikipedia.org/wiki/Paul_Dirac

Yet this beauty and elegance cannot be measured in any numerical way or to any degree of accuracy as the term accuracy is commonly known. A mathematician just knows that it is correct merely by its elegance. An elegant proof excites a mathematician. It makes them feel good.

2. The Mathematics Used in Describing the Quantum World

Plato, who was born in 427 BC and died in 347 BC, wrote:

> The reality which scientific thought is seeking must be expressible in mathematical terms, mathematics being the most precise and definite kind of thinking of which we are capable. [15]

It is clear Plato was not talking about numbers or merely the geometry of straight lines, curves and circles, nor about equations but more about mathematical thought which eventually led to such concepts as Groups, Rings, Fields, Vector Spaces etc.

We do not intend to go into any mathematical technicalities, but the reader might be interested in knowing the broad areas of mathematics which is used in describing and analysing the Quantum World. We can all remember the 'imaginary number', the square root of -1, which was introduced to us in secondary school. It is denoted by the letter 'i'. It is called imaginary because one cannot comprehend any number which when squared (multiplied by itself) gives the answer -1. Some would even go further and say that no such i can exist as it is impossible to get a minus answer (<0) after squaring any number. And of course that is correct if we limit ourselves to the Real Numbers. But if we

---

[15] http://plato.stanford.edu/entries/plato/

expand the Real Numbers to include i, all multiples of i and sums of these multiples with other Real Numbers, then we can build up a whole new number system (the Complex Number system) and then explore the properties and characteristics of this new number system.

All of us were introduced to the circular functions of Sine, Cosine and Tangent in secondary school. In college days some of us were introduced to that strange number called the Natural Number, denoted by the letter 'e' that has the approximate value of 2.718. The function $y=e^x$ (the Natural Exponential Function) has the peculiar property that when differentiated it remains unaltered. Some of us may also remember the hyperbolic functions which are defined in terms of the natural exponential and when first introduced do seem very strange, and a typical student often wonders what possible practical application these strange functions could have.

Well, it is these very same hyperbolic functions, together with the circular functions enveloped within the structure of a Vector Space over the Field of Complex Numbers that describe the Quantum World.[16] Any good student of mathematics will not be surprised to learn also that it is using the tools of Calculus within these structures that one is able to explore and analyse the Quantum World.

---

[16] Leonard Susskind, *Lecture Notes,* Stanford University, http://itunes.stanford.edu/

3. The Fuzziness of the Quantum World[17]

But the most intriguing aspect of the Quantum World is the fuzziness and the uncertainty of anything in this world, and so it is here that the mathematical tools of Probability take centre stage. In the Quantum World it is impossible to 'pin down' any 'object' or 'thing'. Rather than talk about an 'object' or a 'thing' in the Quantum World we talk about a photon. There is no common language which can adequately describe what a photon is. Objects, as we know them, have fixed properties like mass, however, a photon is mass-less. To oversimplify enormously, a photon is a tiny wave or particle of light. They are ideal for experiment as they can be seen as light and detected on an x-ray film. Photons and electrons behave in a very similar fashion. In talking about a photon we will be using the term 'photon' to represent all other 'things' which exist in the Quantum World like an electron. It is impossible to have complete knowledge of a photon, that is to know its velocity and it position at any one time. Once its position is known, its velocity is unattainable and vice versa. Particular states (known position and known velocity of a photon) only potentially exist with specific probabilities. There is a specific probability attached to any potential existence. This 'fuzziness' makes many scientists uncomfortable and it does not fit the traditional moulds. However, as the English proverb says 'The proof of the pudding is in its eating', the proof of the real existence of the Quantum World is in the development of Quantum Computers. It is predicted that (for specific tasks and when fully developed) the computing power of one quantum computer will be greater than the combined computing power of all the computers presently in the world. The development of quantum

---

[17] Leonard Susskind, *Quantum Theory Lectures,* Standford University, http://itunes.stanford.edu/

computers is in its very early stages. However, there are crude versions of them in existence at present which tap into the potential contained in the Quantum World. We will say more about quantum computers in Chapter 7.

Chapter 6: Science and Quantum[18]

1. Wave or Particle[19]

According to the understanding of the middle world, a wave and a particle are two different things and are governed by different laws. However, in the Quantum World a photon is both a particle and a wave at the same time or at least it behaves like a particle and a wave at the same time or some may say it behaves sometimes like a particle and sometimes like a wave. It is impossible to 'pin it down' to both position and velocity. So it is characterised by potential and possibility and probability. It is why we say there is a lot of fuzziness and uncertainty inherent in the Quantum World. Photons do not obey Newton's Laws of Motion or any other particular laws of the middle world.

2. A Bundle of Energy in Relationship[20]

We cannot treat a photon as a mere particle. Probably, the strongest statement that can be made is that it cannot be isolated or, put it in another way, it exists only in relationship. Maybe relationship is how it can be defined or best described. We have to leave behind the standard notions of mass and motion and consider the possibility of describing a photon as 'a bundle of energy in relationship'. Are the building blocks of all of reality merely relationships of energy? The precise science of measurement and exactness seems to be totally inadequate to describe this reality of relationships of energy.

---

[18] Marcus Chown, *Quantum Theory Cannot Hurt You*, Faber UK, 2007.
[19] http://www2.slac.stanford.edu/vvc/theory/quantum.html
[20] http://www.science.uwaterloo.ca/~cchieh/cact/c120/quantum.html

3. Einstein's Theory of Relativity[21]

Taking the scientific and mathematical jargon out of the Theory of Relativity of Albert Einstein, basically the theory says that nothing exists in isolation but that everything depends on everything else. Notice how this differs greatly from the mechanical model where different parts are isolated and then analysed and examined. The Theory of Relativity (everything is relative) seems to correspond with much in the Quantum World. Einstein's famous equation $E=Mc^2$ where E denotes energy and M denotes mass while c is a constant (speed of light) is essentially saying that energy and mass are merely different faces of the same reality. This is far from our common notion of mass and energy. It seems, like the fish in the water that are unable to see (conceptualise) the whole lake, we too are limited in our vision. Our everyday language which is based on our everyday experience of reality is incapable of describing the bigger picture, the 'bigger lake' in which we live.

4. Einstein and Mathematics

Mathematics can describe to some extent this 'bigger lake'. Einstein does so in mathematical terms using four dimensional vector spaces and within this framework he is able to outline, predict and measure accurately the motion of stars and planets. The three dimensional geometry which we all learned at school is not adequate to describe the time-space continuum which Einstein describes nor is it adequate to describe the 'curvature' of space which Einstein has shown is effected by the force of gravity. We, with our limited vision (like the fish in the water) see time and space as two different realities. Space, in our eyes, is fixed and time is continuously passing. However it is not like that, it only

---

[21] http://en.wikipedia.org/wiki/Theory_of_relativity

appears to us (in our limited vision) to be like that. Time and Space are merely different faces of one reality. Science fiction films sometimes borrow from these concepts and to a strict rationalist these science fiction films may seem to be outrageously far from reality but in fact they may be far closer to reality than we may care to admit. We are now beginning to realise that during the past couple of centuries we have been exposed to an excess of rationalism which has blinded us to the bigger picture and to greater realities.

5. The Mystics always had a Glimpse of these Realities

There has always been a strong connection between Philosophy, the Mystics and Mathematics. The Mystics, often with a strong philosophical background, merely by meditating, through silence and through stillness, have been able to come in touch with a deeper reality (deeper than the realities of the middle world which we experience with our five senses). Their writings on their experiences of these deeper realities are now corresponding with realities which are being discovered in quantum physics and quantum mechanics through the tools developed by mathematicians. And so now it is all beginning to come together, what the mystics say, what the scientists say and what the mathematicians say. Some of these convergences will be developed further in Chapter 8.

Chapter 7: Experiments in Science

1. The Double Slit Experiment[22]

The Double Slit Experiment is a clear case where the rationality of Aristotelian logic breaks down completely. Here we see one photon going through two separate slits at the same time! One 'object' in two different places at the same time! This, in quantum terms, is referred to as 'a superposition of states'. And furthermore, after the one photon goes through two slits, its presence in two different places allows it (the single photon) to 'interfere' with itself and to act like a wave in motion! Our first reaction is disbelief. But remember the fish in the water; they cannot see the whole lake. Our minds are too small to see much of the bigger picture. Science is now inviting us to transcend the ordinary everyday picture of reality, to go beyond our everyday experience and to get a glimpse of the bigger picture.

2. The Entanglement Experiment[23]

The concept of Entanglement opens up infinite possibilities of connectedness and relatedness. It has been proven that it is possible to connect or 'entangle' two photons in such a way that even if they are later separated by vast distances (even distances as large as light years), making a change to one photon will instantaneously effect the other photon. This 'entanglement' is completely beyond our understanding, yet it is real. It seems that reality will always be greater than what our minds can grasp. It is impossible for us to grasp how connected literally everything is. To bring out this connectedness and interconnectedness it is

---

[22] http://www.doubleslitexperiment.com/
[23] http://www.youtube.com/watch?v=BWyTxCsIXE4

symbolically (maybe realistically!) expressed in the idea that a butterfly flapping its wings in one of the rain forests in Misuku can have an effect on a tornado in Mexico![24] That is how related everything is. Again the science based on isolating items is blown to pieces. Rather relationships and how things are related is the paramount issue if we are to have any proper understanding of reality. The scientist who cherishes interaction, inter-relatedness and connectedness is the one who will most probably reap the richest rewards and come to a fuller understanding of whatever he or she is seeking.

3.   No Such Thing as a Neutral Observer[25]

The most amazing aspect of the Double Slit Experiment is the effect on the experiment when the scientist tries to identify which slit the photon goes through. Observing the wave pattern of the single photon, it is clear that this single photon must pass through both slits. However, once the scientist actually looks at the photon passing through a slit, then it passes through only one slit!!! The photon ceases to act in a wave like manner and now acts as a pure particle, as a pure object of matter and once again obeys Newton's Laws of Motion! The act of observing changes the manner in which the photon behaves. So the idea that the observer can be neutral is also blown to pieces. There is no such thing as an objective or neutral observer. The observer scientist is actually himself/herself an integral part of the experiment. If the scientist wishes to see the photon act as a wave, it will act as a wave and if the scientist wishes to see the photon act as a particle, it will act like a particle. It depends on the observer scientist; whatever he or she wishes to see is what will be seen!

---

[24] James Gleich, *Chaos, Making a New Science*, Penguin New York, 1987.
[25] http://www.youtube.com/watch?v=DfPeprQ7oGc

4. Quantum Computers[26]

The unbelievable phenomena of a single electron existing in two different places at one time and 'entangled' electrons acting in unison are now finding practical application in the middle world with the development of quantum computers. A classical computer has a memory made up of bits where each bit (an electrical charge) represents a '0' or a '1'. A quantum computer has memory made up of quantum bits, called qubits, where each qubit (an electron) can represent both a '0' **and** a '1' at the same time. Notice the emphasis on 'and'. This is possible because of the 'superposition of states'. The real computer power associated with quantum computing is seen when one considers that two qubits can represent all of four states simultaneously, three qubits can represent all of eight states simultaneously, four qubits can represent all of sixteen states simultaneously, ten qubits can represent all of one thousand and twenty four states simultaneously while in the classical computer ten bits can only represent one state at any one time. Just imagine the number of states possible with 100 qubits! A whopping 2^{100} states! Since in the Quantum World one cannot observe directly an electron without interfering with it, scientists are circumventing this problem by looking at an 'entangled version' of the electron. This obviously is a simplification of all that is involved in the development of quantum computers which is very much in its infancy. But crude versions have been tested. In 2009 researchers at Yale University in New Haven, Connecticut, USA, created the first rudimentary solid-state quantum processor. The two-qubit superconducting chip was able to run elementary algorithms. Another team, working at the University of Bristol in the UK, also created a silicon-based quantum computing chip and was able to

---

[26] http://www.sciencedaily.com/releases/2010/01/100110151331.htm

run Shor's Algorithm on the chip. Shor's Algorithm is an algorithm developed for quantum computing which factorises any number.[27]

5. The Potential of Quantum Computers

Shor's Algorithm is important because it is expected that it will have the potential, using a quantum computer, to break the widely used public-key cryptography scheme known as RSA.[28] The security of the RSA cryptosystem is based on the assumption that factoring large numbers is computationally unfeasible. However, Shor's Algorithm shows that factoring is efficient on a quantum computer, so an appropriately large quantum computer can break the RSA cryptosystem. This large quantum computer is yet to be developed.

6. Post Quantum Cryptography Research at Mzuzu University

Practically all present day security in information, (in particular passwords or PIN numbers) is based on RSA type cryptography. So the development of quantum computers obviously has huge implications for e-commerce and banking institutions. It will render all RSA like cryptography useless. There is, however, another cryptosystem called the McEliece Cryptosystem, which is based on a family of Error Correcting codes called Goppa codes.[29] Many feel that this cryptosystem will withstand the power of quantum computing. The reader may be interested to know that Mzuzu University students and staff are in the forefront of researching this family of Goppa codes.

---

[27] http://en.wikipedia.org/wiki/Shor%27s_algorithm
[28] Douglas R. Stinson, *Cryptography; Theory and Practice,* CRC Press New York 1995
[29] John A. Ryan, *Irreducible Goppa Codes,* PhD Thesis, University College Cork, Ireland, 2002

Chapter 8: Implications of the New Science

1. The Relatedness of Everything

Section 3 in Chapter 7 shows that the connections and relations between the observer scientist and the experiment are mind boggling. Again we are thrown back on the relatedness and inter-relatedness of everything. In earlier chapters we saw that nothing exists in isolation. All meaning is found in connectedness and inter-connectedness. It seems that the essential building blocks of everything can be described more in terms of waves of energy and an infinite sea of relationships rather than in terms of fixed matter. The well known dictum 'no man is an island' now takes on new meaning. The electrons and protons and neutrons making up a chair and those making up my body are the same! The difference is in how they fit together and in how they are related to one another. Relationships are supreme. This too has implications for our own lives. It is the relationships which we cultivate which define us rather than 'the things' we possess.

2. A Participatory World

The fact that the photon acts differently according to that which the observer scientist is seeking has very far reaching consequences. In classical science the observer scientist is seen as neutral to the experiment having no effect on the outcome of the experiment. Indeed this is one of the requirements for the experiment to be authentic in classical science. But in the Quantum World the observer scientist is involved in the experiment actually bringing about that which is being observed. The two positions could not be further apart. The whole question of a participatory world is now raised. We are not mere inhabitants of the world but we are participating in the on-going creation / development / transformation / evolution of the world to a far greater extent than we ever realised. This together with the fact that everything is connected and inter-connected makes us humans part of the whole movement towards transformation to higher realities. We are not spectators but deeply involved in the whole evolutionary process. Even without being consciously aware of it, we are involved but the exciting thing is that being aware allows us to be even more involved.

3. Environmental Issues

Being aware brings us closer into the picture. Being aware gives us a greater respect for literally everything. We are now more conscious of how we depend on the environment and if we diminish the environment we diminish ourselves. Imagine what kind of mind we would have if we lived on the moon with no colour, no trees, and no animals, no anything! We too would be grey matter without any colour, without any imagination and without any creativity. It is imperative that we care for the earth, the trees, the fish, the animals, the hills, the valleys, the wetlands, the birds, the air, the rivers, the lakes, and not to forget the butterflies and all the rest. Matters of ecology are paramount in the preservation of live of all forms.

4. The GAIA Hypothesis[30]

The GAIA hypothesis proposes that planet Earth has a life of its own. Like any life it needs sustenance. Like any life if it gets sick it can renew itself if given the space. But like any life, if it is not cared for and is overpowered by negative factors, it can die. We

---

[30] James Lovelock, *A New Look at Life on Earth,* Oxford University Press, 1979.

are coming to realise that we need planet Earth more than planet Earth needs us! Planet Earth can continue without us. In the past planet Earth shook off the dinosaurs, maybe they were getting too big and too destructive of the environment. What about us humans now? Are we getting too destructive of the environment? Cancer, Swine Flu, HIV/AIDS, are these not the result of our 'miss-use' of the environment? Are we going to be shaken off planet Earth? We cannot survive without planet Earth. And so ecology comes into the equation. Care for the Earth comes into the equation. Environmental issues come into the equation. We are all in this together. We need each other.

5. A New Mindset

A new mindset is required if we are to make sense of recent revelations in the Quantum World and related areas. We are enveloped by a universe of enormous diversity and vitality which is alive and pulsating. Everything is connected with everything else. We humans are not masters but rather co-creators. Practically nothing is predictable, rather we are being invited to be open to surprise, expectancy, wonder, creativity, beauty and elegance where the whole is greater than the sum of its parts. The human body which is extremely complicated, made up of so many forces and energies that we cannot comprehend fully, measure in any real way, observe with any great accuracy — like intimacy, the highs and lows of courtship, the excitement of sport, the exhilaration experienced on achievement, the terror of war or the anguish of the loss of a loved one. What is happening in the whole person cannot be analysed nor understood in terms of some of its parts. There is more to it than meets the eye. It is the same with all of reality; the real essence is deep within — more to do with relationships than with objects.

6. New Revelation

Revelation now is not confined to the sacred books but creation as a whole is continually revealing the face of the divine. There has always been the notion that the beauty of nature reflected the beauty of the creator. However, traditionally, theology focused on the sacred books and on tradition. The world was seen as transitory and was not to be taken as serious. There was even the notion of fleeing *from the 'evil world'* in order not to be tainted by it. There is a shift now, especially with the insights of Evolution and Quantum Physics, we now know that the whole universe is just a massive expanding entity, a continuation of the Divine Creative Energy ever present. It is not transitory but part of the Kingdom of God and needs to be taken seriously. Our main function is to marvel and wonder at it all and to continue to sing and dance in unison with it.

7. Redemption of All of Creation

In Christian circles the three wise men coming to Bethlehem with gifts for the infant Jesus symbolise the universality of the implications of the Birth of Jesus for the whole human race, for peoples of all nations and all colours. Maybe, now with the greater understanding we have of the beginnings of the universe and the on-going creation of all that is, we may have a deeper understanding of what St Paul was pointing to when he said "not only we but the whole of creation is in one great act of giving birth".[31] Did St Paul have a glimpse of that possibility that Jesus came not only to save human beings but to save all of creation? Revelation seems to come to us bit by bit. In the Old Testament there was a sharp awareness among the Israelites that God was on their side. The three wise men in the New Testament brought that

---

[31] Romans 8:22

awareness to all peoples, that God is on the side of all peoples. Now, with the advance of knowledge, we are beginning to realise that the birth of Jesus has implications for all of creation. In this context the first Chapter of the Gospel by St John is extremely rich:

> In the beginning was the Word:
> the Word was with God
> and the Word was God.
> He was with God in the beginning.
> Through Him all things came to be,
> no one thing has its being but through Him.

The implications are mind boggling. Who are we to limit the saving action of the Living God? The Dabhar was there before the beginning, there throughout the last 15 billion years and is there today continuing to redeem, to recreate and renew everything. Christmas is surely one mighty celebration of all of this. All that is left for us to do is to sing exultations of praise and glory which are best done in song and dance.

Chapter 9: Our Response

1.   Celebrate through Rhythm and Dance

Movement, rhythm and dance are fundamental in the Quantum World. Literally everything is moving in an elegant dance. The electrons are in continuous motion around their nucleus. Atoms join up with other atoms, all in continuous rhythmic motion, to form molecules and molecules also have their own movement and dance. In the macro world there is also movement and rhythm where the planets and stars are in continual motion, all performing their own dance. In the middle world there seems to be an ingrained compulsion in all things towards dance. It is always a joy to witness animals dance as they express their spontaneity and creativity. We humans also delight in dance to music. Dance seems to touch something very deep in us as if it is fundamentally a part of us. Maybe it is why pop stars like Michael Jackson make such an appeal to us all. We seem to get mesmerised by the spontaneity and rhythm of their elegant movements. We seem to get carried away to a new plane, to new horizons as we become part of the dance. Initially one tries to synchronise one's body movements with the music of the dance and then it is as if the dance takes over and we are then moved spontaneously by the dance itself.[32] We are carried by the dance and its energy, whether bodily or in mind, to a state of unity and wholeness, yet within a freedom of spontaneity and seemingly ordered chaos, to a place of ecstasy. This is why dance is so appropriate for celebrating that Divine Creative Intelligence, Creative Wisdom, Creative Energy, which was there in the beginning, there throughout all of the billions of years of history of the universe, continually creating, continually shaping, continually transforming and still there now,

---

[32]Diarmud O'Murchu, *Quantum Theology*, Crossroad Publishing, New York, 2004, Chapter 4.

continuing to create, shape and transform everything. And this dance, once we synchronise ourselves to it, makes us part of the same movement towards the creation of a new world and the transformation of all that is. Gladly, this dance is still an integral part of African liturgy, African worship and African celebration. This is one of the many areas where Africa can enrich the rest of the world.

2. Mathematics Having the Final Word

It is appropriate in this paper for Mathematics to have the final word. It is interesting to mathematicians that this rhythm, this music, this dance can also be captured somewhat in mathematical structures. Within the music and the dance there is symmetry. Symmetry is always connected to harmony and simplicity and beauty. It was in the pursuit of this beauty in symmetry that the mathematical structure of Group Theory developed. Now with the advent of Algorithmic Mathematics and with the power of computing, this symmetry can be generated into computer images. This is what is becoming to be known as Fractal Geometry. It is far from the dots, straight lines and curves of Euclidean Geometry but exploits the ordered chaos and the unseen symmetry in nature and captures it in a mathematical algorithm form, which can be run on computer. The variety of possibilities in algorithmic form is vast which reflects the true nature of things in the natural world. Again, we see the wisdom of Plato when he declared that

> The reality which scientific thought is seeking must be expressible in mathematical terms, mathematics being the most precise and definite kind of thinking of which we are capable.[33]

---

[33] http://en.wikipedia.org/wiki/Plato

www.ingramcontent.com/pod-product-compliance
Lightning Source LLC
Chambersburg PA
CBHW051617230426
43668CB00013B/2133